# Amazing Bird Builders

## by Carol Pugliano-Martin

## Table of Contents

# Introduction

They don't wear hard hats. They don't use machines. But most animals are amazing builders. Many animals build their own homes. Their homes are structures that shelter them from the cold and the rain. They are also places where they can retreat from danger. Beavers build **lodges**, bees build hives, and birds build incredible nests where they hatch their eggs and raise their babies.

A golden oriole feeds her chicks.

Have you ever seen a bird's nest? Some are made of twigs and are round and shallow. Others are made of grass and are long and deep. Still others are made from mud and look like small cups. There are even birds that use their own saliva, or spit, when they build a nest. Many birds' nests contain feathers and hair. This makes the nest a soft place for their babies, or chicks, to sleep. Birds are some of the most amazing **architects** in the animal world!

This altimira oriole seems comfortable in its large nest.

Robins lay three eggs in their nests.

# CHAPTER 1
# Tailors and Weavers

Have you ever seen a bird sew? You would if you watched a tailorbird. It can stitch its nest together. Tailorbirds use their beaks as needles. They use vegetable **fiber** as thread to sew the edges of leaves together. This makes a little pocket. The bird lays its eggs in this pocket and raises its chicks there. Tailorbirds even tie knots in the thread to keep the pocket from falling apart!

Tailorbirds are found in Malaysia and the Philippines, as well as China and India.

A tailorbird

A male
weaverbird
hangs from
his nest and
makes noise
to attract
a female.

One of the best architects of the bird world is the weaverbird. This bird weaves hundreds of pieces of grass together to make its home. Male weaverbirds build nests that attract **mates**.

Other types of weaverbirds build giant **colonies** of nests. The colonies are like bird apartment houses. In fact, they can house up to 500 birds!

Most weaverbirds live in South Africa.

## CHAPTER 2
# Eagle Nests

Eagles build the largest nests in the bird world. Some can be almost 10 feet (3 m) long! Bald eagles build their nests in the tops of trees that are near water. They eat fish so they build nests that are close to their food.

**Bald Eagle**

Summer range

Winter range

Year-round range

Eagles live over most of North America, from Alaska and Canada to northern Mexico.

Eagles choose high spots for their nests. They can see everything going on around them.

The eagle's nest is made mostly of sticks. The eagles place these sticks in layers. The first layer is made in the shape of a triangle. The next layer is an upside-down triangle. They keep building like this until the nest is finished. Then they line their nest with moss, pine needles, or grass. This helps keep the chicks warm and comfortable when they hatch.

Step 1    Step 2    Step 3

## Big Sticks

Big nests need big sticks! The sticks eagles use to build their nests can be up to 8 feet (2.4 meters) long!

Some eagles use the same nest for up to fifteen years. Each year they add sticks to the nest to make it larger and larger. A nest may start out measuring about 3 feet (1 m) across and 1 foot (0.3 m) deep. Then, as the years go by, it can become as large as 10 feet (3 m) across and 15 feet (4.5 m) deep! A human being could rest quite comfortably in an eagle's nest.

The world's biggest eagle's nest was found in Florida. It was 9 1/2 feet (3 m) across and 20 feet (6 m) high! This nest was probably used for about one hundred years. It weighed more than 2 tons, or 4,000 pounds (1,800 kg)! That's as heavy as a large car!

Eagles lay one to three cream-colored eggs in their big nests.

## CHAPTER 3
# The Bowerbird

Now you know that birds build amazing nests. But birds build other things as well. Male bowerbirds build shelters called bowers that attract females. The bowers are built on the ground. They are little huts made of twigs, leaves, and moss.

After people build a house, they finish the job by painting it. There is one kind of bowerbird that paints his bower too! The satin bowerbird paints the walls of his bower with chewed berries or **charcoal**.

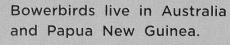

Bowerbirds live in Australia and Papua New Guinea.

A bower is like a stage for a bowerbird. He will dance around it to attract a mate.

Not only do bowerbirds build an impressive bower—they decorate it! These bowers have been known to contain feathers, pebbles, berries, and shells.

Satin bowerbirds use blue. They decorate their bowers with anything blue they can find. Some bowers contain blue feathers, blue pebbles, blueberries, blue shells, and blue flowers. The birds often use human-made objects as well. Some have decorated their bowers with the tops of pens, beads, buttons, and even car keys!

Different types of bowerbirds decorate with different colors. This male bowerbird carries a decoration in his beak.

The more decorated a bower is, the more a female bowerbird will like it.

## Plastic Rings

Milk companies in Australia stopped making the plastic rings on milk bottles blue. These rings attracted male satin bowerbirds. But they were dangerous because they could get stuck around the bird's neck.

# Conclusion

The birds in this book are just some of the fascinating builders of the bird world. Each **species** of bird builds its own special structure. Sometimes it's a tiny leaf pocket sewn by a tailorbird. Sometimes it's a massive eagle's nest the size of a car. So the next time you're outdoors, look up. Look down. Look all around. You may see for yourself an amazing bird builder!

This crane is placing a twig onto its nest.

# Glossary

**architect** *(AHR-ki-tekt)* a person who designs buildings and supervises their construction *(page 3)*

**charcoal** *(CHAR-kohl)* a soft, black form of carbon, made by partially burning wood *(page 10)*

**colony** *(KOL-uh-nee)* a group of animals or plants of the same kind that live together *(page 5)*

**fiber** *(FIGH-buhr)* a long, thin thread of material *(page 4)*

**lodge** *(LOJ)* a beaver's home *(page 2)*

**mate** *(MAYT)* the male or female of a pair of animals *(page 5)*

**species** *(SPEE-sheez)* a group of animals or plants that have many characteristics in common. Members of the same species can mate and have offspring. *(page 14)*

---

# Index

# Comprehension Check

## Summarize

Complete a graphic organizer for this book. Then summarize the information you learned about birds.

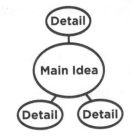

## Think and Compare

1. Reread page 4. What details does the author use to describe the tailorbird? *(Description)*

2. Which nests or bowers mentioned in this book do you find the most fascinating? Why? *(Synthesize)*

3. Many birds build their nests in trees. Yet people are cutting down many forests to build new homes and stores. What do you think might happen to bird populations as a result of this? Why do you think this may happen? *(Evaluate)*